Praise for Dutch Treat

Lively, poignant, funny, and observant, *Dutch Treat* shows us romantic connections, made and missed, and why, even at a Certain Age, they are the heart of life.

— Daniel Menaker, author of *My Mistake: A Memoir*

This book is funny, heart-wrenching in places, and supremely optimistic about aging. It is, in every sense, a tale about connection. About love. About where and how you find it. There is boundless energy and spirited generosity on every page.

— Judy Goldman, author of *Losing my Sister*

Mary Ann Young's *Dutch Treat* is one delectable read! With unapologetic candor and refreshing wit, Young's adventures in dating in her sixties illustrate the surprising ways our human needs and urges refuse to fade as we age. Yet wisdom and experience don't necessarily make romance or relationships any easier. What a sexy, funny and unpredictable literary ride into the golden years.

— Rigoberto González, author of *Butterfly Boy: Memories of a Chicano Mariposa*

Readers seeking clever, laugh out loud, heartfelt short (short?) stories ... your match is here! *Dutch Treat* follows the quest of this smart, sassy author hoping to find her good man. A fun and sincere view of dating while collecting Social Security. Treat yourself!

— TTZalinger, MA, MSW, proud AARP member

Mary Ann's stories are filled with pathos, suffering, and reality mixed with humor. You will arrive at the end of this small book with a deep appreciation for her talent as a writer who has a healthy outlook on life and possesses a keen sense of the ridiculous. In these personal peeks at her life she becomes a person you get to know intimately. You will want to sit with her over a mug of hot tea/coffee.

— Laura T. Jensen, author of *Step by Step, a memoir*

Mary Ann Young's *Dutch Treat* is an honest, unflinching, world-weary look at senior dating that tells it like it is, in all its touching and often hilarious glory. You certainly don't need to be of AARP-age to appreciate Young's candor and camaraderie as she describes her dating exploits.

— Kim MacQueen, author of *Out, Out* and *People Who Hate America*

The author alone is solely responsible for the
content of the book and bears all responsibility for
the publication of this book.

The names of people and some places have been
changed for the sake of privacy.

© 2016 Mary Ann Fuller Young. All rights reserved.
ISBN 978 0 69266 592 3

No part of this book may be reproduced in any form—
written, electronic, recorded, photocopied, or otherwise
—without written permission of the author.

*Senior Dating
& Other Stories*

Mary Ann Fuller Young

Stories

Dutch Treat 11
A Blind Date 19
Ditch 23
Ernie 27
It's Being in Love 35
I See Red 43
Chomping at the Park Lane 45
Room 510 49
The Green Front Door 55
Lazy Bee Inn 59
Click, Click, Click 63
Rookie 67
Hoping For Dessert 71

For you, the men on Match.com and SeniorMeet.com who joined me, and treated me, for coffee or lunch as well as the men who should have but didn't. You know who you are.

Best,
Annylou, alias
Lab pyr, alias

Dutch Treat

I am not so modest anymore.

I am in my early sixties, divorced, in good shape, tall, and slim. Friends describe me as vivacious. Smiles come easily.

I should not be spending my days by myself talking only to my droopy begonias, sweeping the courtyard, or tossing sticks for my yellow Labrador, Barnes.

In the spring I inspect the posh Fearrington Village in North Carolina for a friend and end up building a house there myself. The community is eight miles south of Chapel Hill, composed of mostly unretired retired persons eager to pursue their wide range of hobbies. I jump right in and take bridge lessons, join the golf group, speak out in the writers club, and form a gourmetbee dinner club of eight ladies. My Write Time groups, based on the Amherst Writers and Artists method, gather weekly around my dining room table. Barnes keeps busy insisting that squirrels not play in our yard and watching for the deer that cavort near the back fence.

Writing workshops are my change-of-pace adventures. I am a workshop junkie, traveling to Taos, Santa Fe, Key West, Asheville, Amherst, Durham. Day and night, I do writing practice, writing practice, fast paced writing practice with my favorite, fine point pens as Natalie Goldberg recommended in her workshops. At an

Amherst Writers and Artists workshop Pat Schneider noted, "We use a large amount of energy writing. As much as in having sex." I heard that; it dawned on me that my fast favorite fine point pens and my growing stash of twenty-seven beautiful journals should no longer substitute for a fine, favorite live-in male.

Elinor Jane, a single gal who lives a few doors down the street, recently snagged a handy round-the-house live-in. She is an acquaintance and I don't know her quite well enough to ask where she got him. I see him frequently, weeding or planting pansies or sweeping the driveway. And he grills on the Weber.

Up in the cul-de-sac, a recent widow flashes a one-and-a-half carat engagement ring fifteen months after her husband passed. Pretty fast dancing, don't you think?

Last Sunday was a first and a last for me. Never again will you find me at a fundraiser, sitting with seven smiling dolled up ladies, waiting for artichoke appetizers and chicken Kiev, watching swaying couples on the dance floor. I was jealous. Of the couples. Of the dancing. Of the melding.

As soon as the Independent Paper hits the stands in Raleigh, I scoop up a copy and go right to the Men Looking for Women section. Where are the men past the age of sixty, even in their later fifties? I want a companion of my vintage. In casual conversations with friends, and especially when meeting new acquaintances, I find myself tossing in comments such as, "Well, living alone I..." or "As a single it is..." Automatically, my eye checks out wedding ring fingers, which I soon discover are misleading. I learn that some men's fingers swell, just like mine, and they can't get the ring off. And some men keep a ring as a badge of *something*. I also pay very close attention to obituaries. That is tricky. How soon is too soon to approach a recent widower and offer meatloaf, mashed potatoes, and chocolate chess pie?

I find a phone pal in the Singles Meet Singles ads in the local paper. His name is Houston, but I call him Texas. He is seventy-one years old, a Duke graduate, part-time accountant, mostly in tax season. He lives on the second floor of his sister's house in Greensboro, cooks his supper on a hot plate, has an under-the-counter refrigerator and a big screen TV. He is so damn straightforward it is disarming. Texas determines that I needed some loving.

"Do you like kissin'?" he asks.

I say we could meet and go for a walk with Barnes in the Duke forest.

"Do you like huggin'?" he asks.

He says he can be right over as soon as I give him my address and he gets his truck out of the shop. His sister has been hinting at buying him a new car, but it would have to be a big one, he says, seeing as he is over six foot three and a bit hefty at two hundred and thirty pounds last time he was at his doctor's office.

In a couple of days, he has a car and is coming to Durham for a Phi Beta Kappa meeting and can meet me to see if we like each other.

"How about Shoney's up there on Hillendale for coffee?"

I ask if the invitation includes lunch. He hems. More hemming.

"We'll have to see if we like each other."

Durham may not be the culinary capital of the South, but it seems to me that a Duke man ought to be able to come up with some place a cut above Shoney's and, anyway, I don't like feeling that I am on display for his approval, like a heifer at the state fair. Plus, I think he is slinging bull.

I find hope. A couple at the Chapel Hill Senior Center bridge games discovered each other at Match.com. I go straight home and sign up for the reduced rate, six-month plan. Satisfaction guaranteed, they claim.

The first thing you do for Match is fill out a detailed profile about yourself. I am almost rigorously honest while also attempting to sound like a game girl, flexible and willing to participate in a prospect's hobbies, excluding bird watching or motorcycle rallies. In my teens, I was sometimes described as a flirt. Surely, I can awaken and utilize that attribute now and be appealing to the numerous men I expect to respond to my profile. It is easy to create my profile.

Height: 5'6" (down from a lofty 5'8")
Weight: slender
Hair: silver grey
Age: see comments below
Marital Status: divorced
Education: degree
Hobbies: willing to explore and discover
Financial Status: o.k.
Smoking: No
Additional comments: My age is middle sixties but I feel more youthful. I cook, but would rather "assemble" prepared foods from Healthy Living or a high-end deli and add some personal touches, like white grapes to chicken salad or a slab of Swiss cheese on a veggie burger. Not everybody loves dogs but I do so I mention my brilliant, gorgeous yellow Labrador, Barnes.
Favorite places to visit: the beach, the woods, big cities.
Favorite activities: movies, theatre, concerts, visiting ethnic restaurants, walking with my brilliant, gorgeous yellow Labrador, reading. Would dance if I could find a partner.

In addition to my profile, I describe the man—men—I want to meet: someone with similar interests, loyalty, availability, and financial security. He is trustworthy and willing to spend his money on me, but I don't put that part in. Match.com strongly recommends that you include a photograph. A friend snaps my picture until we get one that is just right, with an inviting come-on-over smile.

The job of Match.com is to send me profiles of men who fit (very loosely I might add) the description I had submitted. I check messages constantly, before breakfast, after breakfast, in the afternoon, after dinner, before bed, to see if Mr. Suitable has responded to my profile and sent me a wink or a message. The winks are generic messages such as "You are a fave," "I'd like to hear from you," "I dig U." I don't use winks. I send personal messages, thoughtfully crafted, confident that I can demonstrate my desirability and elicit a response. If the prospect does not respond within a short time—a couple of days—I delete him. Prospects who use code names such as Rarin' Romeo, Here for U, Prince and Charm, Biker 44, are instantly scratched from my inventory. I figure guys who choose those names are pretty full of themselves, you know?

The Match.com process of waiting to be chosen brings up memories of Miss Cohen's ballroom dancing school in Fairfield, Connecticut, in sixth grade when the girls lined up against a wall and the boys charged across the room and bowed to you to request a dance. I prayed for some kid tall enough so the top of his head did not hit me at my budding breast line.

It is my theory that the easiest way to discover if I and my potential match have any interest in each other is to meet for coffee or lunch as soon as possible and not spend a lot of time writing back and forth with messages on Match.com.

The first man I agree to meet picks a restaurant that makes the best tuna fish sandwich on the East Coast, so he claims. He is leaning on his car, wearing a navy blazer with five tarnished gold buttons, and a pale blue dress shirt, open enough to reveal sparse, fuzzy, blondish chest hair. One black loafer has lost its tassel. No socks. His best tuna fish sandwich restaurant went out of business two years ago and has been replaced by a deli that doesn't do tuna on Tuesdays. We are there on a Tuesday. No Socks grumbles over his chicken salad on white with no lettuce, no mayo, no slaw, no fries. Water. No mention of dessert. My attempts at conversation elicit no more than a yes or a no, period.

It is useful information to see how a prospect handles the bill. I offer to pay my share, but I hope he will insist on treating, as had been the custom when I was growing up. No Socks pays my three dollar and sixty cents lunch bill.

"Thanks."

I am in my car and heading home in less than forty-five minutes. Delete No Socks. Sure, I knew he had written me off as I stepped out of my car, but it still feels good to push the delete button. The next prospect lives on a golf course (good), was widowed four years ago (okay), towers over me (nice), and is very attractive (possibility here). As soon as we slide into the restaurant booth, he starts with a barrage of questions. It is an interview and he barely pauses for my replies.

"How long have you been doing Match?"

"How long have you been alone?"

"Did you marry, have children, where are they, how old are they?"

"What are your favorite activities aside from sex, HAHAHA?"

After he learns I was divorced twelve years ago, he says, "I think I'll stick to widows. They won't have all the baggage you have."

Finally, he quiets and gazes at the ceiling.

"I do miss sex, though," he says. "The more I can get the more I want. You know what I mean?" A pause.

There is no chance I say anything here.

"I'm true to my woman, though." He drinks half a glass of water.

"Serial sex. That's what you mean," I quip and surprise myself with the sassiest grin I can dig up.

For the duration of lunch (he orders tuna fish salad, no bread, and I forget what I have, but it is not tuna fish), he describes the Baptist moral code that was his upbringing. I guess the Baptist code is on the shelf now, but I don't care enough to ask. No mention of dessert. He pays the bill. As I slide out of the booth, he swishes his hand over my fanny. At my car, he grabs me for a very tight bear hug. Such nerve. Apparently I am not chosen to be his one and only, even temporarily. Apparently he assumes he alone can make that choice. Delete, delete, delete.

You might think I would quit the game. Not me. Mr. Suitable is surely about to materialize in my inbox any day now.

Emails are written and phone calls made with the next Match.com prospect for two or three months before I agree to meet for lunch at the beach in Wilmington, halfway between our homes. Barnes goes with me. He likes surfing the waves and rolling in the sand, so the two-hour drive will not be a bust. In his profile, this match says that all his life he's been told that he looks like Sean Connery. And he really does. There is not a thing wrong with that. A tantalizing tic flickers at the right corner of his lip. I want to touch it. His dark brown eyes are stunning. He sports a proper salt and pepper beard, well-groomed. Before retirement, he had been an archery coach and took his team to the Olympics a few times. Impressive. When I learn he has been on and off of Match.com for ten to twelve years, I wonder what is amiss. He had a wife, he explains, who kept running away to the city lights in New York.

While waiting for lunch, Mr. Sean Connery Look-a-Like comments that he is ready to sell his condo in Myrtle Beach and move anywhere; get in his truck with his fishing gear and bike. He adds that he putters, gardens, fixes things around the house, and likes to cook. He eats seven to nine walnuts every morning. It sounds like he is applying for a position. Handy man? Live-in? He has had ten to twelve years of practicing this speech. I forget to ask about the importance of the seven to nine walnuts because our luncheon plates arrive. Sean Connery Look-a-Like invites me to Myrtle Beach, to see the sights. We can sneak my dog into his condo, since he is president of the condo association and has an end unit. It occurs to me that the Myrtle Beach sights might just be his condo. Halfway through the cottage cheese on his Henrietta's Happy Health Plate he says his testosterone is climbing rapidly. I suggest we stop at the Fudge Factory up the street on the way to the parking lot. (Okay, that was a pretty lame reply but what would you have said, and you know about fudge, right?) He pays the bill.

And then blah… blah… blah…

He emails me about a visit to Myrtle Beach. "I promise to behave," he writes. Smiley face. A week or so later, I phone him to postpone the invitation. Silence. He hadn't readily recognized my name.

Delete.

At long last, a really good profile shows up. Joe, a semi-retired veterinarian, did obedience training with dogs for search and rescue, has a few master points in bridge, attends church almost regularly, likes to dine out. Anticipating an invitation for a white linen napkin luncheon, I settle for meeting him at Manhattan Bagels in Raleigh, as he suggested.

"I'll be wearing a red carnation," Joe says.

I spot him right away, all skinny, five foot three of him. What's a few inches between friends? Anyway, I like wearing flats. And what's wrong with towering over your male companion? Movie stars do it all the time.

Joe picks out a day-old plain bagel, requests house water, turns and grins at me, pays his bill, walks off and seats himself at a window table while I wait at the counter for my everything bagel, toasted very dark, with light cream cheese, extra butter and jam, and an endless cup of coffee. Despite Joe's interesting credentials, he is dull and the conversation is stilted, gets stuck on where we grew up, what we do in our spare time. I get a vague invitation to a matinee movie on some Saturday. He offers cheese and crackers for a picnic in a park or in the car if it rains. "Do you crave dessert?" he asked. Who would ask such a question? I ramble on with too many excuses about how busy I am and on and on and so forth and so on out the door and goodbye, Joe. Yes, I am busy. I have to throw sticks for Barnes, watch him chase squirrels, tend to my dying begonias, sweep the courtyard, and cancel my remaining few weeks of membership with Match.com.

A Blind Date

Randolph invites me for lunch at Southern Seasons in Chapel Hill at 12:30 p.m. I am twenty minutes late. That is unusual for me and, looking back, I can only say my resistance was at play. I can't spot Randolph, and I certainly am not going to wander through the restaurant looking for him. What kind of gentleman wouldn't wait at the front door or at least leave a message with the maître d?

As soon as I get home I call Alice, who arranged the date, and learn that Randolph has already called her. He wondered if I really wanted to meet him. The miss-connect never gets explained and "shouldn't bother us," he says. A couple of days later, he phones and invites me to the upscale Sienna Restaurant and gives me explicit directions as to its location, which I know but he doesn't ask if I know so I don't tell. Some guys need to feel knowledgeable and helpful. Dinner is from 7:00 p.m. until 10:00 p.m. He talks. I listen. He talks.

Next time we meet he says, "We have a lot in common." I listen. At that dinner date he keeps ordering more tea and only briefly dips the tea bag into his cup. Extravagant, I think. He could have just requested more hot water. "Ran," as he prefers to be called, rambles and fills the spaces with "let me ask you this." It is nice that he asks about my opinions. I would like to have more moments to voice them. He is, indeed, different.

I begin to wish his phone calls were more frequent.

On our fourth date we go to the Lantern, a wonderful but noisy pan-Asian restaurant in Chapel Hill. Ran speaks over the din and launches into a soliloquy before his appetizer arrives about why he would never marry again. His speech goes on through duck soup for him and seared tuna tower for me. I think it is presumptuous of him to assume someone would want to marry him. I don't say so. I know why he feels it is necessary to tell me this and I chuckle inside. Somewhere before the end of dessert he concedes that it is not wise to say never. I take home a smooth pebble from the decoration on the side of our booth and put it on the window ledge by my kitchen sink, next to the good luck magic eye that Alice brought me from one of her exotic trips.

We continue to see each other for movies, lunches, and Sunday night Chinese dinners. We walk close together and bump. I get a message that he doesn't want to hold hands.

Ran has deep black eyes that suggest something secretive and mysterious. I carefully avoid making comments about his considerable bulk, much of it settled in his belly. He begins a workout program at Duke Center to increase his strength, improve his core, and fix his posture and gait. He continues to favor his right side. Proudly he tells me he is "star of the month" at the gym. The tiny grin that plays along his lips makes me want to kiss him. He doesn't like to wear his horn-rimmed glasses, which I tell him make him look like Richard Gere (it is a stretch), and he hates his seatbelt. He is sixty-five, sometimes going on seventeen and that is when I like him best.

We meet frequently in a parking lot in Chapel Hill because it is halfway between our homes, and his driving is atrocious, so I drive most of the time. After a date he sticks his head through my car window and gives me a peck on the cheek. Toward the middle of June, Friday night before I am going to visit friends in Hilton Head for a week, I say, "Gimme a kiss."

"You got it," he says.

Sloppy. Wet. On the cheek. Through the car window.

I call the next morning and learn he is packing for a trip to a spa in Sonoma. His doctor says he needs to go. Ran has been having more serious back pain and is taking strong narcotics. That explains his slurred words. I hate waiting out long pauses as he tries to complete sentences and express ideas.

"Ran, when would you have told me?" His trip means that he is not able to accompany me to the Fourth of July party at my neighbor's house as planned, nor would we go to the fireworks in Cary. I ask about our plans to go to Kiowa Island. He says that tomorrow he will call the travel agent and book some time. That's what he said last week. And a month and a half ago. I suggest the 7TH to the 13TH of September. He sums up with the 14TH to the 21ST. What do you suppose the chances are of this trip happening?

"I'll call you on Saturday morning." The phone rings Tuesday at 4:30 p.m. His voice is clear, not the garbled, slurred voice he had during the period he was trying to get his meds adjusted for his pain and whatever other ailments he hasn't told me about. "I am practicing my oratory skills," he says. It is nice to hear from him and I tell him so. Also that he was supposed to call on Saturday. "It's Saturday here in Sonoma," he says. Ha.

"When will you be home? I miss you. Quite a lot, actually."

"Come to Sonoma. We can tour here and then I will take you for a cable car ride in San Francisco!"

"I will give it some thought," I say.

What will I wear? Do I have air miles? What's on my calendar that needs postponing?

The phone rings. Ran explains that his plans are changing and he is headed to New York to see his ailing brother. Or is it his ailing cousin?

Suddenly I know I am standing under an apple tree, waiting for a peach to fall.

Ditch

I oughta do that.

I've been saying that to myself every time I pass the sign advertising the farmers' market, Thursdays, 3:30 p.m. to 6:30 p.m., in the rural town of Pittsboro, North Carolina. It's time I check out this local scene.

The natives call me a transplant. I think of myself as a grown-up Cosmopolitan City Girl from Northwest Bergen County, New Jersey, an upscale area popular for its easy commute to Manhattan. Ask around and you'll see how many people now living in North Carolina are from New Jersey. A sizeable number of us live equidistant between Chapel Hill and Pittsboro in Fearrington Village, a sophisticated community for mostly "mature persons, with get up, go, and wherewithal." Seniors flunking retirement.

My transition from New Jersey to North Carolina has been easy. On the rural roads with a Toyota Tacoma pushing 60 mph and kissing my bumper, I enjoy cruising by the tobacco fields and farms. Golden Oldies are blaring for my private sing-a-long.

Oh, what a beautiful morning...
Oh, what a beautiful day...

Thursday. I arrive at the Pittsboro farmers' market, 3:15 p.m., ninety-seven degrees. Muggy. A few customers milling around, some cars, more trucks. I am heartened by what look like peaches. Hope to find local corn. I accept that my neighbors choose to harvest tobacco instead of corn. In August I go to Vermont. Off the beaten paths I am surrounded by sunflowers and corn that can be six feet tall.

The market is set up at the old fairgrounds, a little east of the town circle. I swing my 1995 Subaru off the gravel road, a smooth driving maneuver I practiced fifty years ago when I was learning to drive a four on the floor. My practice area was a double wide sloping driveway lined by five foot tall stone walls. I had free rein within the driveway and strict instructions not to graze the walls or the lolly columns in the two-car garage. Grandpa sat in his red leather armchair in the den above the garage gazing at the checker game in front of him, but I knew he was tuned in and listening for a crash. It was his car, his lolly columns.

At the market, I back in next to a dusty white Volvo. Sure, I gloat over my ability to judge the proper distance and line up perfectly parallel on the first swing.

Oh. Driver side, rear, sinking.

Oh. Car in ditch.

Glad that I am wearing a bra on this hell hot day, sorry that my yellow short shorts are more appropriate for gardening than for being in public, I slink out of my car. More customers arrive and drive on by to a safer parking area.

A blue Outback with a crunched right front end slows as I stand and dumbly stare at my rear end.

"Are you a savior sent to help a damsel in distress?" I ask, taking in the peppered beard and rumpled head of matching hair. "It was stupid. Didn't even look behind me. Thinking about peach crisp, corn pudding, and what all I might buy."

"Welp, we'll have to see here," he informs me. "Yup. Have a look here. I, um, recommend that you look where you are going."

I scuff the dirt with my right foot. Smooth my too-short shorts. Squint into the stunning sun. Sense a sliver of a grin on his weather-worn face.

"Tried a go?"

"Huh?"

"Tried to ease her on out?"

I guess he figures if I am stupid enough to get in the ditch, I am stupid enough to stay in the ditch.

"Oh. Sure. I tried. Spun the tires, the wheels, burned rubber, pushed air."

I move in closer to his old Subaru. A gnarled cane, wooden, leans on the passenger seat. His well-fed belly protrudes between parallel navy blue suspenders. Large workman's hands rest on the steering wheel.

Have I combed my hair?

He drives off to park his car in a safe spot, gets out slowly, and ambles over with a slight limp, no cane, and goes to my rear end. Driver side. He tells me to get in, put her in low, and go.

"How low?" I ask. *Geez, what a question. Is there no end to stupid?* Aha. Forward movement.

"Hold it, hold it," he yells.

I feel the eon it takes to get my foot off the accelerator. I look back. Savior Man is in the gravel beside my car. Prone.

He speaks. "You're dragging the barricade."

"What barricade?"

He assures me he is not injured, just embarrassed. He smiles. Upper right molar missing.

"Guess the barricade didn't work." I giggle. Now I can see a sphere of white concrete tied to a flimsy wooden stake very much stuck under my car.

Prone Savior Man asks for a hammer. Not a chance in my car. Just maps, dog toys, Sugar Daddy candies. His right leg stays straight as he struggles up and limps over to his car to get a hammer. He gets back down in the gravel and commences to slug away at the barricade. He tells me that it is wedged tight by the muffler and the struts and he wants to fix this without doing any damage to my undercarriage.

"That's good. Good."

I watch beads of sweat line up on a bald spot before they run off and get lost in black and grey curls. I resist the urge to wipe his head.

Success. My car is freed from the barricade. I offer to buy him an iced tea or such from who knows where. He declines. We shake hands. I babble thanks, gee, thanks.

"I'd advise you not to do that again." His large amber eyes scan my face. I look away.

I head for a new parking spot, barely miss the ditch on the other side of the road. It is small in comparison, but still a ditch.

No peaches. No corn. I buy wildflowers and promise the vendor I'll return the jelly jar container.

The following Thursday, 3:15 p.m., I return. A "caution" sign is stuck where I went in the ditch.

I look for peaches. Search for corn. Hope for a blue Outback with a crunched front right end.

Ernie

"What's your wildest sexual fantasy?" Ernie asks as he sinks into my new, extra firm, cream-colored leather sofa and reaches to put his hand on my thigh.

One Sunday afternoon at the Raleigh ballet, my friend Winnie pointed out a heavy-set man standing near the stage. She knew I was single and looking.

"That's my friend, Ernie. He likes to do things, you know? Like you. He's good for movies, dinner. Can buy what he wants. You know what I mean? I could give him your phone number, but only if you say so."

I didn't say anything.

Winnie added, "He's looking for someone who likes to dance."

That was the clincher. I imagined myself in a swishy, strapless, burgundy satin gown with a new seamless Victoria Secret Cleavage Creator and here is my Fred Astaire, albeit with a fifty-inch waist.

Ernie is a lawyer, likes travel, dining, theatre. Divorced, he's been living alone for eleven years. I cannot deny that Ernie is good company. Entertaining. An amusing storyteller. He opens doors for me if I stall a bit. He promises trips, adventures, dancing. Every bit a lawyer, he talks a lot, explains a lot, covers the bases. I don't expect that to change. There is never any holding hands, or kissing, or patting on the tush. Not even a hand on my shoulder, for that matter. Will *that* change?

Four months later, after a few ballets, numerous movies, many meals, a couple of concerts, but no dancing yet, Ernie is at my house for dinner. I set out two large linen napkins so that he can tuck one under his chin and over his belly, Godfather style. Crystal, polished sterling, loin lamb chops (three for Ernie and one for me), asparagus, buttered Yukon potatoes garnished with bits of parsley, and homemade chocolate chess pie. Then hot water with a dip of an herbal tea bag and two and a half packets of Sweeta for Ernie. Black coffee for me.

Two hours later, on to the living room. The lights are low and the fireplace crackles. And so, Ernie sinks onto my new, extra firm, cream-colored leather sofa, reaches to put his hand on my thigh, and inquires about my sexual fantasies. He acts blasé. A lightning bolt heads toward my chest.

"You don't have to answer now. Think. You can think about it."

My voice escalates in pitch as I sputter and say I don't, um, think, um, at all. I forget what I tell him. My tongue is glued to my upper lip. I don't think to ask about his fantasies.

After a while longer and more talk by Ernie, he ambles toward the closet for his well-worn, brown tweed jacket.

"Thanks for the evening. Will you come to Asheville, and stay at the Grove Park Inn with me? See the foliage. It's a good year, I hear."

"Absolutely."

I am a sucker for a road trip, besides which the Grove Park Inn is posh with a capital P and their spa has a five star rating.

The following morning an ad catches my eye in the AARP news bulletin.

Enhanced Sex for Seniors. Satisfaction guaranteed.
Free, a year's subscription to the popular magazine
<u>*Sexual Freedom for the Mature and Handicapped*</u>
if you check the box below.

I check the box.

Money back, no questions. Mailed in a manila envelope.

I pay extra postage for overnight delivery.

Ernie phones to say he has to postpone the leaf trip. He suggests we spend the weekend at a local bed and breakfast where he had at some point attended a catered dinner affair for a Georgetown Law School reunion. He adds that he plans to visit the Adam and Eve store for some tapes we could watch on "sex after forty."

"How about sex after sixty-seven?" I ask.

"Hey, wait a minute. I'm only sixty-six."

Friday morning Ernie arrives, bent, very tilted.

"Put your bag on the back seat. My back is sore. Can't lift anything," he explains.

"Why not in the trunk?"

"My things are there. We'll be stopping first at South Point Mall. I want us to pick out some videos together, then we'll be going to Mario's Chocolate Shoppe."

Our final destination is thirty, maybe thirty-five miles from my house. I settle in the front seat and note that Ernie has directions from MapQuest. The car smells faintly of rose petal deodorizer, the kind they use in some ladies' rooms. I wonder how many tapes we'll watch and when we might start, but I don't ask. At f.y.e. Music Store, Ernie chooses four classic song-and-dance romance movies. Fine with me, not that he asks. At Mario's, the new Italian Chocolate Shoppe that has rave reviews in the local papers, they are offering free (miniscule) samples for the month of October. I stand by the assortment of truffles while Ernie claims he is a connoisseur of fine chocolates and negotiates for extra freebies from Mario himself.

The bed and breakfast, an elegant 18th century plantation home, is nestled in mature magnolia and pecan trees on acres of lawns and gardens, just off Route 85 in Durham, North Carolina. Rotund pumpkins and red, black, and yellow scarecrows are tucked around the wicker furniture on the wide, pillared porch. The hostess scurries out to greet us as we drive onto the gravel driveway.

"Welcome, traveler. Welcome," she chirps as she approaches the car and offers her help. She smiles, then grimaces, as she tugs Ernie's suitcase out from the jumble of laundry baskets, lawn chairs, and file boxes in the trunk. Marmalade, the elegant, well-fed house cat, pauses her grooming and moves off the porch step to slide under a bush. I get my small overnight case from the back seat and offer to carry the square red leather 1950s style cosmetic case that Ernie says has to go in. Later I see that it is chock full of meds, labeled on the lids with masking tape. His leather monogrammed Dopp kit has what one might pack for an extended international trip: one hard and one soft bristle toothbrush, toothpaste, nail file, dental floss, hair brush, shampoo, shower gel, body lotion, shaving things, two brands of powder, all of which he lines up around the sink. Our large, first floor room—previously a parlor—is the prize of the Inn. Recently renovated, it has a canopied, king-size bed, with puffy, pink and pale purple pillows, a tiled fireplace, and a basket of starter logs. Extra wood is stacked on the patio outside the curtained French doors. The down comforter is featherweight. On the mahogany tea table lie current magazines, best seller books, Thin Mint candies in their individual paper jackets, pens and stationery, teas, coffees. The Jacuzzi is a notable attraction and I envision a lovely soak for us.

"Lunch. What time is lunch?" Ernie inquires.

"We serve breakfast, Mr. Broadman. 7:30 a.m., bright and early enough for you, I hope. We serve until 9:00 a.m."

"Dinner. What time is dinner?"

"Breakfast, Mr. Broadman. Bed and breakfast, and I am sure you will enjoy it."

The hostess's eyes disappear as she poses and beams. "And here is your room key and a key to the Inn. We lock our front door at 9:00 p.m."

I half expect her to curtsey.

"Breakfast," Ernie mutters, shakes his head, and goes to brush his teeth. He comes back grinning, turns the tub's white porcelain faucets on full blast, peels off his clothes. In my opinion, no male over the age of twelve should consider wearing no pouch white cotton underwear. Ernie does. It sags from his waist. Still smiling, he watches, closely, as I neatly fold my clothing and slowly undress. I climb into what is, at best, a Jacuzzi for one and a half. I get a new understanding of "fantasy" as naked Ernie dips his toes in and then hovers over the soothing warm water and me. Below his swaying belly, his equipment reminds me of the dimmer switch in my dining room.

"Hot."

"You can get used to hot," I tease. Water sloshes over the sides of the tub as Ernie laboriously maneuvers in. We are snug, like two large peas in a little pod.

Our hostess neglected to warn us that the Jacuzzi will rumble and back flush thirty minutes after we use it. Together we bounce on the canopied, king-size bed where we rest until Ernie is over his hot spell, caused by the very short time spent in the heat of the Jacuzzi, or so he claims.

I am anticipating an upscale luncheon and have a swishy new dress for the occasion. Ernie consults with our hostess about restaurants. We miss the luncheon window at the local tablecloth restaurants and are pointed in the direction of a Subway that is easily accessible. When we get there, Ernie rummages in his back pocket for a coupon for a free sandwich.

"Pick out something for dinner," he says as he hands me the coupon. "We won't be going out again."

We eat in a booth next to Route 85, a major truck route that points north. I hear about Ernie's exploits, the big money cases his law firm wins, his racquetball games, high school sex explorations. He is good at talk.

Back at the bed and breakfast, Ernie sits on the side of the bed and reads the newspaper. I stretch out on the bed and leaf through the magazines, wait. I light the fire but it keeps going out. I use all the starter logs. After an eon we sit in the wing chairs for our sub supper. Ernie has turkey on whole wheat, dry—in keeping with his new diet—and I have a mushy tuna wrap and a limp pickle. Ernie remembers the chocolates from Mario's and a bag of Snickers that are in the car. He puts the one-size-fits-almost-all white terry cloth robe over his Fruit of the Looms. The laces on his Reeboks dangle. He drops a key into the robe pocket.

"Bye."

"Bye."

I move from the wing chair to the bed. It seems he is gone a pretty long time. I sense that he is locked out of the Inn. I imagine him ringing the bell, banging on the door to rouse the hostess to regain entry. As soon as I hear a key touch our room lock, I open the door. The comforter I've wrapped myself in slips, revealing my nude shoulder. Walking in, Ernie peels more of the wrapper off his king-size Snickers and offers me a bite. I take the whole thing.

"Time to spoon!" he announces with gusto. To me, spoon is a verb, as in to cuddle, to neck. We climb onto the bed, toss some of the pillows on the floor. Ernie arranges me next to him. Pulls me closer, a la spoon. Spoon. A noun. He throws his right arm over me, and is snore-roaring in less than two minutes. The unending night is punctuated with Ernie's periodic nasal outbursts.

At the first whiff of bacon, Ernie is off the bed, swiftly dressing, out the door and at the breakfast buffet. While I am sipping my coffee, our hostess wants to know where we are from, what we do, where we are going. I smile. Ernie chews. I pause. Quietly, I mention research, confidentiality, and the importance of privacy. I smile again. She bounces away to enthusiastically welcome an exhausted-looking newlywed couple.

Ernie is going strong spreading raspberry jam on the boysenberry crepes when I ask for the car keys and say I will get a start on loading up. My overnight case is packed and ready. I add a pen and a few Thin Mints from the tea table in the room to my purse.

"Thank you," I say to the Innkeeper in the entrance hall. He appears confused as to why I am leaving abruptly.

"Mr. Broadman will need a cab, if you don't mind. Thank you." I adjust the side view mirrors on his BMW, hook up the seatbelt, discover reverse and bump, not too severely, into the wide, pillared front porch, sending Marmalade scurrying under her bush. At the end of the gravel driveway, I ease onto Route 85, tune into the classical station on the stereo, and head to Asheville.

It is a good year for foliage.

It's Being in Love

I have exchanged my jeans and loafers and stay-at-home mom garb now that my son is off to college and I dress for success in my busy real estate career. Francis commutes from our hometown in New Jersey to his position as a senior vice president in a well-established executive search company in Manhattan. Most people call him Frank but we have agreed that I may refer to him by his birth name, Francis. It fits him perfectly, I think.

Around us in the year 1984: Ronald Regan is president and gets reelected with fifty-nine percent of the vote. Murder, She Wrote and Jeopardy debut on television and are colossal hits. Apple introduces a user-friendly personal computer. Twenty cents buys a first class stamp.

Francis and I are acquaintances in A.A. We meet often before and after meetings to talk. I like that he asks my opinion on things. I like that he is so honest and straightforward and is willing to listen to my gripes and challenges as I work to quit drinking. He makes me feel important. We become good, close friends.

On a drizzly and cold February Friday, I drive to the Rosedale, New Jersey, train station. I am dressed for Manhattan, in a navy blue suit, a crisp white linen shirt, and a long, swirled red and orange scarf. My black leather boots are comfortable for walking.

I am nervous about traveling alone, excited about the adventure. Will Francis be waiting for me at the door to the 68TH Street Presbyterian Church to go to an A.A. meeting? I buy a newspaper, choose a window seat, watch commuters board and get off at the many stops along the way. I tuck the newspaper under the seat and stare out the grimy windows into suburban backyards with naked trees, dried up leaves, scattered toys from warmer days.

I find Francis and we join the crowd of people awaiting a small, clunky old elevator with a black lattice safety door. It settles into its first floor niche and we politely move in, turn to face forward, and adopt the standard elevator gaze. At each floor the elevator slows, laboring with its load, then it gets a burst of energy to lift upward and continues to the fifth floor. The noontime meeting is about the promises of A.A. Close to a hundred people are in attendance.

After the meeting Francis says, "I have made a reservation for us for lunch at the Rockefeller Plaza if that suits you. We can watch the skaters."

"Thank you. Sounds lovely," I reply.

We are about the same height and easily fall into synchronized step on our way to the restaurant. The waiter at the Rock Plaza greets Francis by name and nods at me. After lunch Francis firmly takes my hand to cross the street and he doesn't let go. We walk to Schrafft's to indulge in a banana split with a sea of gooey fudge sauce and three red cherries atop a mountain of whipped cream. Francis picks up one of the two long-handled silver spoons and offers me the first mouthful. He smiles at my unconcealed happiness.

I like to look at him. He is distinguished looking, has a tiny scent of spice. A solid sort of guy, broad shoulders, played fullback in high school, ice hockey in college until, to the dismay of his teammates, he preferred membership in the drinking club. He is immaculately groomed and always has a red or white silk pocket square in his blazer breast pocket. I tease him and ask if he irons his handkerchiefs. His arms are ready to open; a laugh waits on his lips. There were cascading blond ringlets in his little boy pictures but now he is balding and greying at the temples. His eyes, a deep hue of powder blue, tantalize. He cares about me and I bask in the attention. He cares about others, too, and does hospice work. He holds doors for strangers, would tip his hat if he wore one.

"When will you come back to the city?" he asks, in the middle of the banana split.

"Soon," I say. You betcha, I think.

Francis pays the luncheon bill, like he always does, at the swanky King Cole Bar with one of the ten or eleven credit cards that he carries in his left pants pocket, wrapped in a wad of pink memo slips secured with a rubber band.

"What's with the wad of memo slips?" I ask.

"They tell me who calls, what they say, what I say," he explains.

"So, you have a portable office."

I pull my coat close to my chin in anticipation of the chilling February wind and head towards the elevator. He follows me, closer than usual. Uncomfortably close. I tap the elevator button on the brocade wallpaper. The door slides back. As one, we move into the cherry walled cocoon. I glance up at a burned-out bulb in the gaudy chandelier. Francis moves in for a kiss. It surprises me. And I am a willing participant. Bells ring from impatient patrons on the upper floors of the hotel, but Francis locks the elevator. We'd had fleeting pecks on the cheek at holiday times and birthdays in the past, but this is the first real kiss. It doesn't matter that we are in our fifties. A first kiss is a first kiss.

One crisp and crystal clear day in early December I am catching snowflakes on my tongue while we stroll on Madison Avenue. Francis invites me for lunch on Valentine's Day. It's curious that he issues this invitation so far in advance. I am flattered.

It isn't so important to me, but Francis mumbles that he should have made a reservation when we arrive a few months later at the Café d'Artistes and our usual table—number twenty-one in a private alcove—is not available. He steers me to the bar to wait. The cashews are fresh and addictive. We sip Perrier.

After perfectly poached salmon, blanched snow peas, watercress and endive salad, Francis peers over his horn-rimmed glasses, focuses into the distance over my right shoulder and says, "I don't know how to tell you and…" My insides collapse, my face pales, as my first reaction is fear that he is moving away or is gravely ill or is announcing some other pending disaster. But, I hear, hear him say, "I am in love with you and I have been trying to tell you that for a very long time."

This twist in my life makes me giddy. I can't stop grinning. I can not speak.

'S wonderful, 'smarvelous, that you should care for me… The song lyrics breeze around in my head on my train ride home. Now I can hardly wait to tell Francis about my feelings, but I will wait so I can tell him in person, when we meet again.

It is teeming, teeming rain as I ride in a cab at the pace of an earthworm across town to meet Francis. I would be walking briskly, maybe running, if it weren't for the wind and rain. The second I see him, beneath a huge black umbrella, I bolt out of the cab, dash through the deep puddles by the curb, and jump (as well as a fifty-one-year-old girl can jump) into his black chesterfield coat and declare, for the world to hear, "I love you, I love you! Do you hear?"

There is much I do not know about Francis; we know what we tell each other and what we see in each other. We both had long-term marriages and have grown children and grandchildren. I love what I know about Francis. I love what I can see.

We are walking, arm in arm, on the way to a concert at Lincoln Center and we are close to Francis's office where he has worked for more than ten years. He stops abruptly at a corner, shakes his head and says, "I'm confused. Don't know which way to go." I read the street signs to him and he reacts as if he has never heard of Columbus Avenue.

He laughs it off and says, "It's being in love!"

More and more frequently Francis can't locate the memo he wants out of his wad of papers, his portable office. It doesn't seem to bother him as it would me. When we are living together I notice that he uses all his different credit cards and pays only the minimum monthly due on the escalating debt. I discover that random letters, not full words, are filled in on the New York Times crossword puzzle that he always carries. Phone calls become more frequent. Conversations become repetitive. Blank moments occur.

I arrange doctor appointments. The diagnosis is probable Alzheimer's. Francis is fifty-six years old. Some would say he is in the prime of his life. We muddle along and muddle along. We take long car rides and slow walks together, always holding hands.

It is another December, wholly different than the one years ago in New York City, and I tap the elevator button on a smudged, beige wall. I ride in the ninety-degree capsule with a nurse's aide and a terminally ill woman slumped in a wheelchair, her head almost on her knees, a small pink bow fastened to her snow-white hair. I am going to the Alzheimer's Wing at a care facility in Chapel Hill, North Carolina, where loved ones are "safe and secure."

I walk down the hall, trying to avoid looking through the wall of interior windows. Sometimes I stop and look in at the patients, like people often stop and look in at the newborns in maternity wards, and I see Linda, standing at the wall, unable to figure out how to turn around. Someone will come along and turn her. She will walk off until she gets stuck at another wall. I see Norman, pacing in a circle. Henry is half toppled out of his wheelchair, a sign that he will leave soon because the patients must be mobile to stay in this wing.

Eighty-year-old Ginger struts around, fidgeting with the buttons on her blouse, eager to show off her imaginary baby. And where is my Francis? Many times I forget the code to open the door even though I used it the previous day. Today, I succeed in getting in. I call out "Hello," ask for my Francis, listen as the cheery aide assures me he is here somewhere, just went by on a walk, just went somewhere for whatever. Often I find him alone, in someone else's room, napping. Or he is slumping in a green, plastic recliner, next to other slumping residents, in front of the television set, while a game show host wearing a bow tie offers wild and wonderful vacations and prizes to lucky winners.

Francis wears baggy sweats now and someone else's plaid shirt. His shoes don't match. He was such a dapper dresser that I am always a bit shocked when I first see him like this. When he was still at our home and dressing himself, he started putting two or three sweaters on, one on top of the other, in the hot and humid North Carolina summer until I wised up and packed his out of season clothes out of sight. He also redressed several times a day. I asked him about this behavior and he shrugged his shoulders and smiled his beautiful, infectious smile that reached from yesterday to tomorrow.

His decline is rapid. Is that fortunate in a disease where prognosis is only downhill?

In the beginning days in the Alzheimer's wing, Francis shaves and dresses himself. He offers to sweep the halls. He talks to other patients who rarely answer. Perhaps, when people live together like this they build a communication system, without talking, that the rest of us don't understand.

Some days I have to wake Francis and a slow process of recognition begins. His eyes squint, then open wider. His mouth forms a little O, a precursor to a squeaky whistle or just a push of air. On a good day he puckers up for a kiss. His shaky hands come up from his lap to his chest and reach out toward me. I kiss him. I walk into him and hold him for a hug. His somber blue eyes pierce me.

Some spouses hang out, it seems, all day, walking, feeding, dozing with their loved ones. They sing songs for recreation. "Take Me Out To The Ball Game." "Give my Regards to Broadway." "Itsy, Bitsy Spider." There is a beautiful atrium attached to the Alzheimer's wing, but I never see anyone use it. It is kept locked. I ask for it to be opened and Francis and I sit on a wooden bench amid the trees and flowers. I hold his hand. It is impossible for me to stay very long. I figure Francis has no concept of time. But I know he knows I am there. He puts his arm around me or reaches for my hand to walk me to the locked glass door when, in preparation for leaving, I jabber about the errands I must, simply must, do. The aide helps me with the code to get the door open. Two or three times Francis tried to maneuver his way out with me, long, long ago, in the beginning days. He has been in the Alzheimer's unit for fourteen months. It seems like a lifetime. When the glass door is between us he waves bye-bye, spraying his individual arthritic fingers like an old-timer waves to attract a baby's attention.

I cup my hand to my chin and send forth a stream of butterfly kisses and call out,

"I love you, I love you. Do you hear?"

I See Red

I see red. Everywhere is red: cupids, bows, arrows. Red velvet heart boxes filled with luscious chocolates ride in white and gold Godiva shopping bags. Valentine hearts dangle in space.

And the heart pins. You always gave me heart pins. Different sizes and different shapes but always hearts, wrapped in sparkly white tissue paper. I will never know if you knew how many heart pins you gave me. Christmas. Valentine's Day. My birthday. Did you forget your previous gifts? Perhaps so. You wanted to show me your love over and over again.

The pins are in a Wedgewood candy dish on my dresser.

I am wearing my skimpy red nightie that I bought to be coquettish with you, how many years ago was it? And I am propped up against all the puffy pillows that you loved to fling on the floor before we turned out the lights. And I am alone in our king-size bed that we shared for so many nights, so many days. Might as well have been a twin bed since you always rolled close to me. I can almost hear your breath, feel your warmth, your softness. We had the fat cat, Sagamore, to accommodate on the bed with us, too. He doesn't come around since you've been gone.

I tumble into jumbled memories. They catch me like a loosely woven cotton hammock and surround me so that I cannot scatter. I hold still so as to not tip over and spill.

Buds are on the trees. You planted tulips out by the woodpile.

"Don't plant them upside down, like you did with the carrots," I joshed.

You looked at me and grinned.

Sometimes you sucked in air, with a tiny whistle, and I would ask what you wanted to say.

Silence.

I get out of bed, pull a sweater over my nightgown. It is misting—spritzing, you would say—and I walk out to look for your tulips. Crocuses, purple and yellow, are poking up through the earth, determined to make a statement.

In my heart I hear you: *Enjoy your journey. I am waiting for you.*

The greening of the grass and the budding of the trees are comforting. My eyes crinkle, my nose twitches, my tongue touches my teeth. I smile. I imagine you walking, hesitantly, towards the woodpile to greet the tulips, the gladdening harbingers of spring.

Chomping at the Park Lane

"Come to room 1418," he tells her when she calls him on the hotel lobby telephone. "The door's not locked."

She opens the door to the suite and puts her new purple roll-along suitcase in the corner. Elegance surrounds her. High ceilings, moldings within moldings, mahogany-colored leather furniture. A bouquet of perfectly formed pink and white roses, bigger than she could imagine.

"I'm not doing very well," he calls out by way of a greeting.

Ten days previously he'd settled in at the Park Lane Hotel in New York City to get yet another opinion from a heart specialist. He'd been to the top honcho in Durham, (City of Medicine) as well as to the chief of the cardiovascular department at the University of North Carolina.

"Sorry," she says.

He continues to sit by the window and leans upwards for the kiss she plops on his overgrown salt and pepper hair. There is a thinning spot by his left ear. He readjusts his gray sweatshirt over his belly and shakes his head.

She is miffed because she was overcharged by the cabbie, on her circuitous ride into the city from the airport and didn't think to get the driver's identification number or the license plate information.

If she tells him about it, he will expound, expound, and expound on what she should have done.

She goes to the bathroom. His grooming products—Biotene Oral Rinse, Jack Black Turbo Body Wash for Athletes, Johnson's baby powder, Axe Wet Shine Spray Gel—are scattered amid Zantac, Gelusil, Milk of Magnesia, and Clif energy bars on the beige marble countertop.

"I've been thinking," he calls out. "It may work."

"What will work?" she asks.

"May. I said *may* work. Relationships. Relationships take work."

She sits on the ottoman next to the pile of rumpled newspapers and smiles at him. She figures he is telling her that he takes work. Right.

"If it is a good relationship and people fit together it isn't work or anyway it doesn't feel like work. With my Francis it wasn't. It didn't feel like work," she says.

"He had Alzheimer's."

"Before the Alzheimer's. Are we going out? What about dinner?"

"We'll eat here. Enjoy the view. Central Park. It's raining."

"It's September. It could rain more. What view?" She pulls back the freshly laundered sheer curtain and peers into the fog.

He starts in again. "What do you expect?"

"For dinner? For what?"

"For our life. I find it's good to jot some things down. It doesn't have to be an encyclopedia. Just jot some things down."

"How's your heart, anyway? What did the doctor say?"

"It's thumping."

He grins. She thinks he is trying to look sexy.

"I waited for you to get here," he says. "We go to the appointment in the morning and then have lunch on the East Side and then we can have a long nap."

Whoopee, she thinks, musing on the visit she was anticipating in the Big Apple. She gets her purple roll-along suitcase and goes into the elegant bedroom, takes off her new deep green suede wrap skirt and coordinated cashmere sweater set, kicks off her high leather boots, and wiggles into the black lace and velvet thing.

On the morning of her birthday last month he'd phoned and asked her to meet him at Victoria's Secret in the mall. He wanted to buy her a birthday present. While she was browsing at the display of matching pajamas and robes, she, and all of the customers in the store, heard him ask a salesperson, "Do you have anything transparent?"

"I pick something for you and you pick something for you," he'd explained. He grinned a big one and paid for her pink rosebud pajama and robe set and the black lace and velvet thing.

That same day he had told her, "I am a lover of New York City, the Broadway Shows, Sardi's, the Cotton Club, Village Jazz. I can show you the town." She had heard every bit of that very clearly.

She sashays barefoot around the room in her transparent black lace and velvet thing. The underpants piece is like a Doritos on a string. Binding. But it's part of the outfit he bought for her. She hums some of "Stompin' at the Savoy." *Your lips as warm and sweet as wine...*

"By the way," she asks, "what about that Christmas present from last year? What's up? Anything?"

His special big surprise Christmas present to her had been his plan to consult about an implant to facilitate, no, guarantee an erection.

"Doing research. Considering different angles."

"How many angles can there possibly be? Seems you do a lot of that. Research."

His glasses on the tip of his nose, his pen on the New York Times puzzle, he asks, "What's a seven letter word for Central American lizard and please call room service. Burger. Rare, very rare, veggies, no salt, no butter, Diet Coke, make that two, apple pie, heated."

"I guess we're not going out in the New York City you love. No "Stompin' at the Savoy?" Just chomping at the Park Lane? Hello, room service? Yes. I'll have the fillet, very rare please, baked potato, loaded, but everything on the side, avocado endive salad, dressing, yes, on the side. For him… maybe lizard."

She hands him the phone.

Room 510

"The way you do this," he said as if I had asked, "is you stand with your back to the fountain and with your right arm toss the coin over your left shoulder. And make a wish." He handed me three coins.

It was dark when we arrived at the travertine stone Trevi fountain in the center of Rome. White lights twinkled from the Carrara marble statues—well-endowed muscular men with curly hair—that embellished the famous fountain. The crowd resembled one at Lourdes, without the wheelchairs and crutches, everyone hoping with a toss of a coin their wishes would come true. People politely stepped aside to give us space at the fountain's edge. With my first coin, I wished for a wonderful nine days in Rome. Next, I wished for a love affair. With the third coin, I wished for a real orgasm.

Robert, whom I met the first evening I attended the Strutting Seniors singles group in Chapel Hill, North Carolina, told me his wishes. A healthy, happy relationship, a long relationship, more of happy and healthy. I didn't tell him mine.

Wishes can come true. I got real.

"Can we go to that nice fountain again?" I asked the following morning.

"Yes. But first, breakfast."

Robert gave me three coins, one of them a big one. I positioned myself with my back to the fountain and tossed each coin with my right arm over my left shoulder. My hopes were high. When you've had nothing in the sack for years, anything can be an upgrade. I made the same wish with all three coins: for a giant orgasm, a giant orgasm, a giant orgasm.

I got giant. Plural. Hot. Real. Orgasms that went all through me, with splashes of fire, down my legs, up my arms, into my toes, my fingers, and then exploded with white lights flashing out my left elbow as I gyrated, grinned, and giggled.

We didn't have to go back to the fountain.

I don't mind telling you that I was taken by surprise by Robert's invitation. He had gone to Italy for a two-week touring trip with his synagogue and decided to leave the rigorous tour and stay in Rome. It was mid-August, afternoon, when he phoned me.

"Come to Rome," he'd said.

"Call me back. I'll let you know. No. Wait. Maybe. Yes. I can do that."

Robert was medium height, with gorgeous hair that hinted about curling when it was a little long. His attentive, azure eyes said, "Tell me more." He sometimes complained of sore knees and preferred to walk at a slow pace. I told him when he reduces the size of his belly his knees will get better, but you know how it is telling a man what to do. I adored it when he let his playful, flirty little boy come out, when he winked and blew me a kiss across the dinner table. Robert's mind was razor sharp. He was a charismatic conversationalist and a fine dancer. In fact, Sherry, the owner of a ballroom dance studio in Durham, North Carolina, invited him to be her partner in a regional dance competition in Raleigh, but he had dropped out because of his knees.

We had been going out casually for about a year. I didn't think of it as dating. But who can refuse an invitation to Rome? Go for it, girl, my friends, my family, and my gut said. At sixty-six, I was lean and lanky, five foot seven (down from five eight). No longer a bleached blond, my flippy, short hair was *au naturel*, with some purchased highlights. I am Libra, seeking balance and harmony. My astrologer dubbed me dynamic, impulsive, a tiger. I laugh easily and smile frequently.

I went to Rome.

Robert was waiting at the airport gate. He was dressed in whites, as if he were ready for a tennis match. We had our first tight hug, with a real kiss and giant grins, then and there. In the taxicab, he told me he had requested that brunch be held for our arrival and he thought his room was big enough to share.

The porter turned the key and opened the door to Room 510. I was pleased to see a king-size bed instead of two double beds that I imagined were possible in an 18TH century four star hotel on the Via Veneto. We deposited my luggage and headed for brunch, an extraordinary presentation of a variety of eggs, fancy cold meats, sausage, bacon, broiled tomatoes and mushrooms, as well as muffins and breads. The dining room was decorated in gold and peach velvet.

"I usually sleep in a tee shirt and shorts," he said.

"It's okay with me if you sleep in nothing at all."

I slurped some coffee and quickly headed to the buffet to hide my blush.

Later, I learned that Robert had chosen to stay in Room 510 with a king-size bed, a defective air conditioning, and three windows, rather than move to a cool room with two windows, and twin beds. Two large white fans, which only slightly interfered with the magnificent view of the city skyline, were added to the elegant ruby red and gold decor.

Robert offered to draw a demarcation line down the middle of the bed.

"Which side of the bed is mine?" I inquired.

"The middle," he responded.

The following afternoon after strolling in the Borghese Gardens, I prepared to settle into the marble soaking tub. Looks big enough, I thought.

"Want to join me?"

"Here I come," Robert said. "Let me get my glasses." I tried to watch the frilly window treatment shuffle in the breeze as he stripped and tucked his clothes into the sink. He braced his sizable sixty-five-year-old bulk against the wall and gingerly stuck his right foot into the water.

Available space in the tub evaporated as Robert turned this way and that and finally maneuvered himself into the water. I activated the jets. The dribble of Sensual Serenity Bubble Oil that I had put in the tub puffed up. Up. Up. Soap bubbles camouflaged our bodies, cascaded over the rim of the tub and mounted up against the base of the toilet. Robert grinned, parted some imploding bubbles and reached for me. I blew a handful of fluffy suds at him.

"I am gonna stick right here. I am stuck on you," I said.

"That's an Elvis song, isn't it?" Robert knew more about more types of music than anyone I had ever met.

"Possibly, Robert. But I am stuck. On you. Maybe stuck with you. Move off my leg, okay?"

"Sure, sure," he said as he rested more of his bulk on my shin and reached for the brass security bar specifically designed to aid the disabled. For one terrifying moment I envisioned the bar pulling free, bringing the yellow tiled wall with it, as Robert and everything collapsed into the rolling foam on the bathroom floor.

I ignored my throbbing shin, now the color of concord grapes, as Robert slowly blotted me dry with one big towel and then wrapped me close to him in another one. My injured leg would have to be out of harm's way when we entwined on the white linen and lace king-size bed, beside the flickering candle.

"One knot, please," he said as I started to tie the sash on my plush yellow bathrobe provided by the hotel.

"Nooooooooo. No knots, please," he added.

At four o'clock, a knock on the door startled us. Naked, Robert got out of bed with a fair amount of agility. It was the turning of the key in the lock that persuaded him to grab my straw sun hat with the dangly black grosgrain ribbon from the dresser, hold it over his privates, and hide behind the opening door. He stuck his head around and said, "Hello-o-o!" I hid under the sheet.

"Lavanderia, sir."

"Hang it. Take it away. Bye, bye."

"Scusi, sir?"

I can't remember exactly when Robert first said "I love you" but I know he was standing by the door of Room 510, wearing black shorts with a loose elastic waistband and a yellow shirt. He was on his way to the front desk to pick up a fax. He turned towards me and said, "I love you." Numerous times during pillow talk he said the end of Rome was just a beginning.

"I'd like to stay here," Robert said on a Sunday morning.

"Sounds good."

"I mean, here. All day."

"Here? In the room?"

"Hmmm. In bed."

"Oh."

"Breakfast first. It's included, I think."

We left Rome on what we dubbed leap Tuesday pretending the departure day didn't exist. On the way out of our room, I grabbed the bouquet of one white rose and two red roses that Robert bought from a street peddler several nights before. Robert was headed to Washington, D.C.; I was returning to Raleigh-Durham. We kissed goodbye at the airport security gate. Wordlessly, so that I would not weep outwardly, I put the white rose in Robert's outstretched hands.

As I flew towards home, I thought about how lovely it was to nestle together, to line up like spoons. We fit. I would feel close to him as we drifted to sleep and he would pull me closer. Even closer.

On my birthday, I got two bouquets from Robert. One bouquet was of six red roses. The other bouquet was of one white rose with two red roses.

The Green Front Door

The head honcho hustles in and out of my condo at Red Rocks, in Burlington, Vermont, supervising the conversion of the basement into a playroom and work area, the installation of a Jacuzzi hot tub, the creation of a library loft on the second floor, and the addition of a guest room with four skylights and a view of Lake Champlain. Refitting my niche is the beginning of my mid-life overhaul, my personal redo.

I don't like to admit it but a few years ago—all right, fourteen years ago—I started having a serious desire for a companion, a live-in-the-house-with-me male companion. I started dipping into the online dating world. My success on Match.com while I lived in North Carolina was limited; prospects sounded interesting and stimulating in the initial contacts but never panned out. The guys were too smart, too boring, too poor, never too rich, too young, rarely too old. At the time it never occurred to me that maybe the guys were okay and I was the one who had unrealistic, snooty expectations, expectations that they would instantly know that I was a treasure. I quit Match.com. I also quit North Carolina.

Honcho was part of the original construction team for my condo and was recommended by two of my neighbors for renovation work. He is a burly sort, of chunky build and medium height. He has a full head of unruly hair, light brown peppered with gray. His deeply wrinkled, ruddy face conveys a history of carpentry jobs done outside in the harsh Vermont winters. His hands are red and chapped. His nails are dirty for life. Honcho's speech is occasionally garbled and I find myself asking him to repeat what he says. He looks me in the eye when he speaks to me. I resist an urge to turn away. I return the gaze.

The men arrive at my green door in the early morning when it is still dark and bitterly cold. They are carpenters, painters, electricians, rug layers, plumbers, and they have a way about them, an air not of arrogance, but rather of confidence. These men interest me. They wear worn woolen plaid shirts layered over sweaters and tee shirts. There are no coats or scarves or gloves. They kick off their boots in the front foyer. The men cough. They cough from sheet rock dust, paint dust, Marlboro dust, Vermont dust.

I muse, propped up in my feather bed with a cup of Green Mountain French roast coffee. Suppose, just suppose the worker bees who showed up at my door were women. Would I eavesdrop to catch bits of conversation? Would they speak of recipes, and diets, and boyfriends? Might I like to be one of them? I was sent to college to get finished and to become marriage material. Was carpentry or plumbing an option for women in those days?

At dusk one day, I dial the cell phone that I know is affixed to Honcho's hip.

"There's a drip in the basement," I explain.

"I'll be there in the morning," he promises.

"You might want to contact the plumber," I counsel, as if he has never confronted a drip, as if I am the head of operations.

"That is not a drip," Honcho says when he sees the wet basement at daybreak. "That is a leak."

He takes the flight of stairs in double time. I find him squatting by the molding next to the newly installed oak floor in the foyer.

"Balls," Honcho exclaims. "Musta put a nail into a pipe when I done that floor."

Sure enough, we find a culprit nail piercing a copper water pipe. Honcho removes molding. Now we have a stream of water flowing into the foyer.

"What do you say we turn off the main water supply," I suggest.

Later the plumber arrives and explains that the nail must have been hanging at the ready waiting to pierce that pipe, so to speak.

"No telling why it don't leak two weeks ago when we done that hall," Honcho says.

"Yip," the plumber Johnnie adds, "Done that very thing, drove a nail smack into a water pipe, done that I'd bet it been fifteen, maybe, years. Yip."

At 3:00 p.m., I head for a Jacuzzi soak. At 3:02 p.m., I dial Honcho and tell him there is no hot water.

"I'll be right over and fix it," he responds. My hero. He could just tell me where to turn the hot water supply back on. For that matter, I could figure that one out myself, college degree and all.

A week or so later at quitting time, five of the men assemble to arrange furniture in my newly created spaces. I have been looking forward to the completion of this project for days. Honcho takes the television set out of the master bedroom and puts it in the library loft. No reception.

"Honcho is king of cable, you know," the gorgeous, grey-haired, bearded carpenter volunteers. *Who is waiting for you?* I wonder, as our eyes connect and I glance down at his silver wedding band.

Various instructions flash across the television screen.

"Gimme the remote," says the painter.

"Numbers we got, no pictures. Oh, shit, I lost it," Honcho chimes in.

"Set the clock. You gotta do this in sequence. Gotta have a directions book for this," gorgeous carpenter adds.

Everybody gets in the act. I could call the cable company in the morning, I think, but remain silent. I know these men won't quit.

Cell phones on hips chime, as someone wants their man home for supper. The hourly wage clock ticks on. Eventually, channel three, with Marsalis Parsons and the evening news appears.

The men swagger off, closing the green front door quickly to shut out the frigid wind. The scent of the men, a mixture of sawdust, turpentine, sweat, and tobacco lingers.

The next day Honcho pulls up in his shiny black van, blocks the driveway, leaves the motor running to keep the van warm. The guys tease him about being a sissy in the cold. Fluffy white puffs of exhaust are blown away by the blustery winter wind. He hurries in to pick up his final check and to inspect the carpet installation in the new bedroom. In a non-stop sentence, he volunteers that he likes his coffee plain, just cream, sometimes drinks tea, and has an hour to wait before his appointment across the street. We extend hands to shake. It becomes a little bit of a roving hands kind of hug.

"Ah, it was an honor."

"Huh?"

"The hug. The hug. It was an honor," he says.

A warm crimson glow graces my cheeks as I slowly close the green front door. I decide to go to Aubuchon's hardware store to leaf through a Sherwin Williams catalog and pick out a sunshine yellow or perhaps a peach to reface my front door. I could paint that door myself. Sure. Of course, I will call Honcho. Tickle his hip with the jingle of his cell phone.

Lazy Bee Inn

Not a soul down on the corner
That's a pretty certain sign
Those wedding bells are breaking up
That old gang of mine.

All the boys are singing love songs…

On a glorious Vermont fall day, she is cruising in the country in her snazzy new silver convertible with the top down and the radio blaring golden oldies. She rounds a bend and comes upon a small, gleaming white Congregational Church. Its steeple reaches proudly into the cloudless sky. Guests are entering the church; the wedding party is arriving.

Memories of her own wedding day thirty-four years ago clamor for attention as she sails down the hill. The year was 1960. They were twenty-two years old. Couples didn't openly have sex before marriage. He asked her to marry him and she said yes, enthusiastically. He told his family about the plan. His mother strongly suggested the marriage be postponed a couple of years, at least until he finished business school. She would not consider any postponement and declared "wedding in June" or she was leaving, leaving him, the East Coast and going to the San Francisco Bay. Period. There was a lamentable long "thinking period."

The wedding was June fifteenth.

She cried at the rehearsal dinner, maybe because her deceased daddy was not there; more likely because she had had too much scotch. Her mother told her in no uncertain terms to pull herself together PDQ and advised that if one drank scotch with a splash of water there would be no drunkenness. It was the mixers that presented trouble.

On her wedding day, she sat alone and stared at the clock. Her family and the bridal party gathered for a luncheon at Aunt Helen's house. It was unlucky, someone had told her, to see the groom before meeting at the altar on the wedding day so she was sequestered until the 3:00 p.m. ceremony.

The wedding album has photographs of her with him, kissing at the altar, sharing the wedding cake, dancing, smiling, the proverbial stars sparkling in her eyes. The members of the wedding party got crocked and forged their own nights to remember.

A pale pink suit with a matching pill box hat and outrageously high spiked heels was her going-away outfit to leave the reception, dodge the confetti, and head off in her new husband's borrowed Cadillac to a surprise honeymoon destination.

They got out of the parking lot and he announced that he was hungry, had eaten only a couple of stuffed mushrooms at the reception. Hours later they stopped at an all-night roadhouse for a very greasy hamburger and French fries which he stuffed in his mouth. The food disappeared as if a Hoover vacuum cleaner had grabbed it and sucked it up. She made her first just-married mental note: see that he eats properly.

Next to the roadhouse cash register there was a sign advertising rooms available. He inquired. Soon she was hobbling on her outrageously high pink satin heels up a dark dirt path to a cabin. The double bed took up ninety percent of the cabin. Only one person could stand and move at a time.

She gathered up her virginal white lace nightgown and peignoir, slipped on her high-heeled mules with the fluffy puffs on the pointy toes, and took two steps to the bathroom to undress, redress. She emerged, face flushed, anticipating a memorable and full night of lovemaking and found him collapsed under the sheet, in his white buttoned up button-down shirt, head tilted left, mouth hanging open. Night number one.

Early the next morning they got going, going, on and on and on until mid afternoon when they arrived at the Lazy Bee Inn, a resort with a cutesy campy motif. Lots of pine paneling, plaid sofas. A bottle of champagne and two glasses with little white ribbons and flowers on the stems were on the mantle. She eyed the bottle. Her very newly acquired husband headed to the four poster canopied bed with giant lace pillows piled high, stretched out, kicked off his shoes. A long, second toe stuck out of his dark blue sock. He said a long second toe was a sign of royalty.

"It's been a long drive. Time for a nap."

She sat and sat. He napped and napped.

On the path to dinner, she slipped her hand into his. Almost. He jerked away as if he had touched fire ants. "You startled me," he said, and put his hand in his pocket to play with his change.

It is cooler riding in her snazzy silver convertible as the sun is starting to set and her journey into the country ends. She recalls his second cousin's wedding, also in Vermont and on a fall afternoon like this one. It was held in a church similar to the one she had just passed. The newlyweds dodged birdseed and ran down the walkway. The bride's father hired a black and gold horse-drawn carriage, all decked out in white ribbons, bows, and balloons, to take the couple down the hill to the garden reception. First the newlyweds rode across the slopping meadow to the grey stone covered well where they had tossed pebbles and pennies when they were first-graders.

After an assortment of home cooked refreshments she and her then-husband danced the fast numbers. He split the seam in his too-tight, too-short linen pants.

...the boys are singing love songs,
they've forgot Sweet Adeline...
Those wedding bells are breaking up the old gang of mine.

Click, Click, Click

For many years I drive from North Carolina to Vermont and live in my condo at Red Rocks for holidays and summers. When it comes time to relocate to Vermont permanently it takes less than a week for me to find a neighborhood where I would like to live. Ample grass and trees and a couple of ponds surround thirty-four carriage houses arranged in a circle. Barnes can cavort off leash in the large meadow with gorgeous foliage, as far as one can see, at the back end of the circle. Rabbits, deer, wild turkeys, and other rural critters share the location. Two vacant lots are available. Singles are in the community. In thirteen minutes, I can arrive at my son and daughter-in-law's house and visit my four grandchildren. I put down a deposit and live at my condo while my new customized home is built.

The floor plan is senior-friendly, with a large master bedroom on the first floor. I have a Jacuzzi tub. I climb the thirteen stairs to my office in a loft. Beats using a stair master to stay in shape. My favorite place is the three seasons glassed-in porch which soon becomes surrounded by forsythia and overlooks a small cutting garden. It feels like being in a serene tree house.

With no man around, what's the next best thing? On a whim, I phone Barnes's breeder and inquire about a Labrador puppy.

Mercedes, a one-year-old yellow female, is available. The breeder sends pictures so I can see Mercedes facial disfigurations. My granddaughter joins Barnes and me for the three hundred and thirty five mile ride to Frenchtown, New Jersey to meet Mercedes.

Short of stature, Mercedes wears a coarse coat, pale gold like Fels Naptha, a contrast to that of my gorgeous thirteen–year-old, Barnes, his fur like sweet creamery butter. They are offspring of championship Labrador retriever sires and bitches who compete in conformation and have many ribbons and trophies as proof. In some fashion, Mercedes and Barnes are related. After a brief romp around the breeder's yard, Mercedes willingly hops into the trunk of my Subaru, curls up close to Barnes's flank, and settles in. We begin our journey home.

As a name, Mercedes is over for me before it begins. She sits up to check the scenery and catches my eye in the rearview mirror.

"Hello, Lulu," I say.

She cocks her head in recognition of a new name that suddenly poufs into my head and fits her perfectly. Later, I make the connection that Lulu was the nickname for my beloved nanny, Louise.

Lulu's length, from scarred lip to tucked tail, seems too long for a Labrador. She, a pup herself at fourteen months, is still showing signs of birthing (an unplanned pregnancy) eight fat and strong and healthy pedigreed pups the color of sweet sue corn. Black skin surrounds Lulu's mouth as if she had stuck her snout into a pail of soft and sticky licorice. Blackness droops from her eyes too, like a lady of the night's heavy mascara dissolving after long hours of street lit wandering. I tire of explaining, but I respond politely to all who ask, "What's wrong with her nose, her eyes, her face…what happened?"

At four weeks, Lulu contracted Strangles, a rare skin disorder. The breeder worried that she might not survive. Because of her lack of facial fur and disfiguration, as well as red eyelids that are missing pigment and have sparse and spiky lashes, Lulu is a gift to me, free, but a priceless gem.

We arrive home. My priceless gem looks around the living room briefly and scoots upstairs to the guest room, squats, and deposits a little bundle. I do not pretend to understand dogs, but I interpret this as a statement that she is moving in. It is a once-only event.

The skin on the tip of Lulu's nose is so thin when I get her that she comes up bloody after she sniffs and hunts in the brush when we walk (Barnes and I walk, she flies like a gazelle) at Red Rocks Park. Nonetheless, her tail is high and swings gaily like a metronome. A tiny scab develops even before our jaunt is over. At home, I slather her nose with coconut oil.

Lulu invites Barnes to play. He most often indicates nay, turns away. Off she goes, *click, click, click* on the cherry hardwood floors. Through the living room, under a table, down the hall. She comes back, my purple croc held high above her head, sashays around Barnes and then goes again *click, click, click*, strutting in the living room, down the hall to my closet. She returns, parading with my pale blue croc, again held high above her head.

Lulu can dig to the bottom of the toy box to unearth a cow hoof, toss it into the air, catch it on a spin as she gathers it in her soft mouth, and bring it to me. Not to give it to me, mind you, just to show it to me. Lulu, a special kind of retriever.

At lunchtime, on the porch, she wants what I'm eating. I give Barnes his large leaf of romaine. Lulu shreds her piece and discards it. *Not my idea of lunch*, she let me know. Barnes chews his organic carrot; Lulu rolls her carrot over her lips, deposits tiny slivers on the rug, then tries to take Barnes's carrot out of his mouth. He sucks up all the slivers. Lulu's attention falls upon the weary cluster flies that are a fixture of Vermont and hover along the edges of the windows.

Who goes there, Lulu squeals with a high-pitched pronouncement that we must be on guard against a grasshopper that appears by the porch door. Barnes replies with his deep, guttural *boom boom* and heads to the front door. My protection team is always at work. Lulu beats a path from the front door to the back door. She trails Barnes everywhere as he teaches her the ropes, my ropes.

A friend builds a ramp to make it easier for Barnes to get into the car when he can no longer make the jump and to relieve me from lifting him. Barnes's passion is riding in the car.

One Sunday afternoon, six months after Lulu moves in, we are returning from a walk in the woods and I hear, "Come on, Barnes, you can do it. We're almost home." I turn to see my ten-year-old grandson, Toby, repositioning Barnes's backend as he starts to collapse in the snow. Toby gives Barnes a body hug and side-by-side they walk home, slowly.

At suppertime, Barnes turns his head away from his dish of food, something he has never done. I always say he would walk across Egypt for a snack. I offer him his favorite treat—banana smeared with peanut butter—and, again, he turns his regal head away. Later, he lets me know that he wants to stay in the kitchen, instead of sleeping on his bed in my bedroom as he always does with Lulu and me. I awake and know to go to him at two in the morning. He is in a spread eagle position; he lifts his head slightly. I tell him once again, and again, as I have been saying for fourteen years, what a beautiful and wonderful "puppy puppy" he is. From day one I have called him "puppy puppy" in a lilting high-pitched voice he recognizes. I doze briefly then awake to be present at his side. He lets go around 4:00 a.m. Lulu comes in the kitchen. She sniffs all around his body. She licks his face. She curls up close to Barnes's flank and settles in.

An antique grain box sits at the foot of my bed. In it are Barnes's ashes, his fourth place AKC ribbon and the prize money (two dollars) for his first place best of brood certificate, his hard earned ribbons from three, maybe four obedience schools. I miss seeing his head pop up to greet me at daybreak. I settle for faint squeals, sloppy kisses, and Lulu's inquisitive brown eyes the color of fudge saying, *Can we get up now?*

Rookie

Finally, in Vermont on SeniorMeet.com, Rookie44 pops up on my laptop. He sounds very good in his profile, has potential. We have similar interests. We have a phone conversation, which I will tell you about but first I want you to see why Rookie's profile attracted me. He says he is educated and financially comfortable, 6'1", six years younger than I, divorced, wants to travel, is romantic, and can cook. Sounds promising, right? We agree to stay in touch. And the best news is he lives close by. This is critical because night vision is diminished in my age group and I am not interested in sleepovers. Yet.

I get an email from Rookie while he is driving to Florida. He says that he and Shirley are laying over in Cary, North Carolina, for a day or two and that he will telephone me when they get settled in Florida.

Shirley?

I like the Rookie's voice on the phone. He calls promptly at the minute we had agreed upon and I don't remember what we chat about until he tells me about Shirley, a great dame, his best friend, who happens to be on his lap.

Help me with this. Why the hell is this guy phoning me at 3:30 Sunday afternoon before the Super Bowl, yakking about the sunshine and the wonderful house in Florida that he found on the Internet and rented for three weeks sight unseen, with Shirley on his lap, her long legs dangling?

"Oops," says Rookie44, "My pants are wet… and some of my shirt, too."

Now, I know for a fact, that women of a certain age can have a little leakage. They can be drippy, especially if they have neglected certain exercises.

After a much needed moment of silence I ask, "How old is Shirley?"

"She is close to eight, I think. I like her long legs and soulful eyes. She likes to sit on my lap. She's low maintenance, really, and she rarely wets my pants. Honest."

Ooooh. Shirley is one hundred and forty-five pounds of Great Dane. How nice. We can walk our dogs together.

When he returns home, the Rook picks me up at my house to go to Leunig's, a bistro on Church Street in Burlington, Vermont, and a movie. Usually, I meet the guy somewhere, so this is different. He comes to the front door and into my foyer and inquires about my wood floor. I, in a moment of blankness, cannot tell him anything, beyond, "Yes, wood."

Rookie44, Rookie, the Rook is tall, well-built, handsome, with hair, a space between his front teeth, and a seductive smile. He has on pressed grey slacks, a white dress shirt, and a blazer. Collegiate outfit. Be cool, I say to myself as I trip on the front porch. He opens the car door for me. I don't have to stall to see if he will.

During lunch he tells me about his short, one-year marriage. His wife—second wife—complained that the shopping in Burlington was lousy and she ran away to New York City. I don't ask about wife number one. I am busy keeping the flutterings in my stomach under control. I order the house special egg white omelet with mushrooms and red peppers and he chooses a drippy Reuben that I practically drool over. He boxes half of it for his supper.

Rookie coached football at Babson and then retired to run a vacation camp in the Northeast Kingdom of Vermont. Before long I hear what I do not want to hear. He is investigating a seniors living community in Cary, North Carolina.

It escapes me what movie we saw. There is no reason he might sneak an arm around my shoulder or hold my hand like in the dark theaters of high school days.

In my driveway, we say goodbye.

"Goodbye. You are a nice lady."

This hunk is going to have ladies lined up and vying for his attention in North Carolina.

Why did he even bother to take me to lunch and a movie? I think.

I also think: Shucks.

And that's putting it mildly.

Hoping For Dessert

We know that my success on Match.com in North Carolina was limited. I am a New Englander. Born in Bridgeport, home of P.T. Barnum, schooled in Fairfield and New London, Connecticut. And now I have relocated to be near my family in Vermont. Perhaps men here are more my style, more willing to have a look at me. I remain trim, can still touch my toes without bending my knees, can eat an eight-ounce porterhouse, and have room for Pecan pie. My hair is full and fluffy and silver. I walk at a decent clip with my live-ins, Lulu, a yellow lab, and Parker, a Great Pyrenees.

I have graduated to SeniorMeet.com. Now I have different desires. I want a guy who will help me put the too-tight fitted sheet on my queen-size bed, a guy who will enjoy my two dogs as I do and walk them in the rain, a guy who will fix an English muffin for me, toast it very dark, and not say, "How can you eat that charcoal?" He will massage my chronic aching shoulders and not stray from my chronic aching shoulders without an invitation.

Just like with Match.com, SeniorMeet.com has a prescribed list of questions to answer in hopes of attracting a mate: age, height, weight, income, religion, looks. There is space to add what one is looking for in a relationship: serious, casual, pen pal, travel companion, all of the above. I opt for all of the above to see what turns up, but I am not looking for casual and I have no interest in encouraging a pen pal.

And of course, I consider income. The common answer to that question on the profile is "I'd rather not say" and I can buy that. Who wants a potential mate to be attractive just because of money, money, money? I will always offer to pay my own way. Dutch Treat. Then again, if my suitor were an elderly, very veeery elderly gentleman with a veeery sizable estate and needed an heir, maybe we could work out an arrangement. Maybe. If the answer about income is "below $12,000" I am not sending a flirt or a message. That man needs a donation. Upward of $50,000 is okay, and if it's "$75,000 plus," well, you know where I am going with that one.

Another profile question is about number of children. Six is suspicious, particularly if the candidate is not Catholic or the head of an African tribe and never has been married.

I always consider height. I like my man to be at least at eye level. Various amounts of shrinkage occurs for men and women as the years go by. I allow for nominal shrinkage. Assuming we travel together, my man must be able to fit into an airplane seat without an extender. A few extra pounds is fine and, as a matter of fact, I like a more substantial chubby chunk who I can hold on to, someone who enjoys eating. Because we all know that food is a readily available substitute for not readily available sex. Plus, you can share it- food, that is—in public and with an almost stranger.

The space provided for likes, hobbies, and ambitions is where I decide if I will pursue or reject. I check for spelling, grammar, content. I look for someone who is literate, enjoys movies, books, food, food, food, (you know what that means) and someone who seems happy and fit. Pet owners are good. Dogs and cats. No snakes. Goldfish don't count.

By the time I get to the dating scene in Vermont, at the age of 75, I learn that it is not what I want that's important. It's what's available. Despite the harsh reality of that lesson, my modus operandi continues to be to campaign for a get together for coffee or lunch with a prospect at the get-go to check on the chemistry ratio.

Martin offers lunch at the Sports Bar on Williston Avenue. He wears khaki shorts in October, mid-calf white socks, a black and white stripped shirt similar to what referees wear at ice hockey games. His eyeglasses are thick like the tops on the old Ball canning jars and I can't tell if he is looking at me or at one of the six or seven television screens while he tells me about his daily activities. Every day begins with push-ups. He plays racquetball on Mondays, Wednesdays, and Fridays, and tennis on Tuesdays, Thursdays, and Saturdays. I've forgotten what he said about Sundays. He insists on paying for my BLT and reminds me he is a gentleman.

"Oh, dear, I never found out what you do," he says as we part. For good.

Kenny is one of the nicest men I have ever met. And the biggest. He treats me to a leisurely lunch of a monstrous pasta concoction for him and a salad with salmon for me, coffee, dessert, more coffee, at the Ninety Nine, a local restaurant that caters to older cliental, has reasonable prices, serves huge portions, and sends out many doggie bags. His obligatory red suspenders blend in with his plaid flannel shirt. His work boots are well-worn. I guess he wore them while he was working for the state and climbing around to inspect bridges. After lunch, he invites me for a ride in his restored Cadillac the following week and a tour of the cemetery in Barre, known for its ornate and imaginative marble headstones and sculpture.

I learn about the history of the Barre marble quarries from Kenny. He tells me about one wealthy gentleman farmer who had a separate grave dug for his favorite cow so that, eventually, they could rest in eternal peace together. True? Who knows? This *is* Vermont.

Kenny is a real snowbird. Come November, he leaves Barre and heads south until April. He bought a furnished doublewide near Orlando for $7,000, and spends his days walking around in the pool and drinking Diet Coke at the trailer park's Tiki bar. As winter set in, he departed Vermont, and also from me, when I refused his invitation for a lengthy visit in Florida.

I agreed to meet up with Zeke at the Champlain Valley Fair. He lives in a trailer near White River Junction, but will travel to Essex, near Burlington where I lived, to see how his cow that he half owns makes out in the livestock competition. I feign interest and try to understand why he wants to own half a cow that he boards at the other half owner's farm. He says it is a status symbol.

Zeke is a handsome guy. He is wearing a tan trench coat over chinos and a fleece pullover and is carrying a black golf umbrella to ward off the impending rain when we meet. I don't ask about his handicap. I learn that he built a house for a wife, but then discovered he is the wandering kind and needs to move on, and on. Alas, come winter he departs to fish in Florida. In the spring, he returns to Vermont to reunite with his third wife and six children.

It gets cold in Vermont. I buy an electric mattress pad and an ivory electric blanket at Bed, Bath and Beyond.

Just before my six-month SeniorMeet.com membership runs out, I come across the following profile from JussmeVt:

An 82 year old man, from Bristol, Vermont…
A little about me…
would like a lady who loves life and what if offers. not looking for an angel but someone for company, companionship. someone who is not afraid to be herself and allow me the same priviledge. i have a decent home, a decent car and $5.00 in the ban…

I chuckled at "$5.00 in the ban…" And I was curious about the personality who would call himself JussmeVT.

We arrange a date at the Bristol Bakery, a new coffee shop, but he never shows up. He phones and says he hadn't been able to find it. Admittedly, it sort of looked closed from the street side. We agreed on a different venue, Panera, on Shelburne Road, a few days later.

In the parking lot, he saunters towards me, standing tall and smiling and wearing a dark suit, a white shirt with one collar button undone and a nice tie.

"Gee, you're all dressed up," I say.

"I figure I was meeting a lady," he replies. I notice that he pronounces the whole word, all the way to the last "ing." I notice his big, infectious smile.

It is his first time on SeniorMeet.com and he only signed up for the introductory offer. I haven't a clue what we ate but we talk and talk and he invites me to his house for coffee. It is good coffee. He promises to make bread for my next visit. It is good bread. Plain white bread that makes excellent dark toast. He serves it with soft butter.

I like that he is looking for someone who is not an angel and not afraid to be herself.

He lets me be me. I try to let him be him. It suits us just fine.

Acknowledgments

The Champlain College Publishing Initiative with guidance from Kim MacQueen and excellent copy editing from Claire Samuel and Elise Price provided the backbone for this book. The topnotch design, format and cover are due to the talented Martin Simpson. It has been my very good fortune to work with these exceptional creative people. Heartfelt thanks.

To the many writers who have been in workshops with me, I thank you for your encouragement and contributions, known and unknown, for my writing life.

www.ingramcontent.com/pod-product-compliance
Lightning Source LLC
Chambersburg PA
CBHW051957290426
44110CB00015B/2277